Jiu-Jits

By: F. Anderson

Jiu-Jitsu Journal
By: Frank Anderson 2016

ISBN-13: 978-1539020844
ISBN-10: 1539020843

Listen carefully to what I say,
What matters at the end,
Matters today.

- Frank Anderson

Table of Contents

Jiu-Jitsu Journal

By:_____
        Student's Name   Date

Academy:_____

Instructor:_____

Instructor:_____

Lineage:_____

_____

_____

_____

_____

Special Thanks to Supporters_____

_____

_____

_____

_____

How to Learn........

The fundamental concept of learning is simple:

- Search and absorb information
- Mentally think about the information
- Physically apply the information
- Troubleshoot and correct difficulties
- Repeat the process and continue to improve

Three of the things that stop people from learning are: Ego, distractions and brain blocks.

Egos should be checked at the door. Listen and absorb information. Keep your advice to yourself until you are at least purple belt.

Distractions are anything that takes you away from Jiu-Jitsu. There are distractions such as family, career and/or school that may not be avoidable but for all other distractions, get rid of them, focus on jiu-jitsu and learn.

Brain blocks can come from you or from others. It's like a weed in a flower bed that just shows up. No matter where the negative thoughts come from, you must conquer them. Don't let anyone, including yourself, ruin your mental toughness. If you are not mentally tough, you came to the right place. Your mental and physical confidence will build, all you have to do is show up.

Always start with a qualified instructor and then use other forms such as videos and books to enhance your knowledge and understanding.

Your academy should be a place where information is shared and corrected, a place where you can troubleshoot your jiu-jitsu and work through problems.

Thinking about the information absorbed can be things like meditating, day dreaming and of course keeping a journal. Writing things down is another way to build memory. It's also helpful to reflect and never forget where you've come from and where you're going.

Practicing what you've learned by putting your body in motion starts to build muscle memory. Muscles don't have memory but your subconscious is being programmed.

Jiu-Jitsu should be just as fluent as breathing. If you have to think about the position, the move and your opponent's move, you are too late.

Humble yourself, LISTEN and correct your mistakes. Listening is learning and you want to learn as fast as possible. Correcting your jiu-jitsu doesn't mean it's wrong or broken. It just means that you have to adjust the move(s) for you and your opponent. Different body styles, fight styles and scenarios will require adjusting of your techniques and combinations.

Safe Training

Every academy has their own code of conduct and/or rules. This should be followed for everyone's safety.

Be safe, conscious and aware. Part of being a high level practitioner is having the ability to feel your opponent's body and movement. You should be completely aware that you are applying a lock on someone. Inflicting danger is good but inflicting injury may have irreversible consequences. Most practitioners have a day job and a family to feed, so keep it safe.

New guys need to relax. The academy coach has paired you with someone who can easily beat you. This is done so you don't get hurt. The high level guys will welcome you to the gym and allow you to play without anyone getting hurt.

Being clean is part of safe training. Your gi should be clean, your hygiene, toe nails, fingernails etc. should all be maintained. Nothing worse than rolling with a person who smells like the bathroom (1 or 2). Don't walk to the academy bathroom barefoot and then step on the mats. Some academies don't have the space to accommodate separation, but please, do your best to not contaminate the mats.

Open wounds will leave you vulnerable to viruses and infections. This is the same for extreme acne. Be mindful of your health and others.

You are going to get hurt at some point in your jiu-jitsu journey. Identify the difference between pain and injury. Seek medical attention and clearance as needed. If you are injured or are in pain, choose your training partner carefully.

Instructions for this Journal are in the back of the book. We don't need no stink'n directions.

Time to roll !!!!!!!!!!!!!

Date / Time/Total Hrs: _____ / _____ / _____

Personal Training Session Goals:_____

_____

_____

_____

Instructor's Technique: _____

_____

_____

_____

Variations of Technique:_____

_____

_____

_____

_____

Combinations with Technique:_____

_____

_____

_____

_____

_____

_____

Defending/Avoiding the Technique:_____

_____

_____

_____

_____

Reflect on your *wins*:_____

_____

_____

_____

_____

Reflect on your *losses*:_____

_____

_____

_____

_____

_____

How can I improve:_____

_____

_____

_____

_____

_____

_____

Date / Time/Total Hrs: _____ / _____ / _____

Personal Training Session Goals:_____

_____

_____

_____

Instructor's Technique: _____

_____

_____

_____

Variations of Technique:_____

_____

_____

_____

_____

Combinations with Technique:_____

_____

_____

_____

_____

_____

_____

Defending/Avoiding the Technique:_____

_____

_____

_____

_____

Reflect on your *wins*:_____

_____

_____

_____

_____

Reflect on your *losses*:_____

_____

_____

_____

_____

_____

How can I improve:_____

_____

_____

_____

_____

_____

Date / Time/Total Hrs: _____ / _____ / _____

Personal Training Session Goals:_____

_____

_____

_____

Instructor's Technique: _____

_____

_____

_____

Variations of Technique:_____

_____

_____

_____

_____

Combinations with Technique:_____

_____

_____

_____

_____

_____

_____

_____

Defending/Avoiding the Technique:_____

_____

_____

_____

_____

Reflect on your *wins*:_____

_____

_____

_____

_____

Reflect on your *losses*:_____

_____

_____

_____

_____

How can I improve:_____

_____

_____

_____

_____

_____

Date / Time/Total Hrs: _____ / _____ / _____

Personal Training Session Goals:_____

_____

_____

_____

Instructor's Technique: _____

_____

_____

_____

Variations of Technique:_____

_____

_____

_____

_____

Combinations with Technique:_____

_____

_____

_____

_____

_____

_____

Defending/Avoiding the Technique:_____

_____

_____

_____

_____

Reflect on your *wins*:_____

_____

_____

_____

_____

Reflect on your *losses*:_____

_____

_____

_____

_____

_____

How can I improve:_____

_____

_____

_____

_____

_____

_____

Date / Time/Total Hrs: _____ / _____ / _____

Personal Training Session Goals: _____

_____

_____

_____

Instructor's Technique: _____

_____

_____

_____

Variations of Technique: _____

_____

_____

_____

_____

Combinations with Technique: _____

_____

_____

_____

_____

_____

_____

_____

Defending/Avoiding the Technique:_____

_____

_____

_____

_____

Reflect on your *wins*:_____

_____

_____

_____

_____

Reflect on your *losses*:_____

_____

_____

_____

_____

How can I improve:_____

_____

_____

_____

_____

_____

Date / Time/Total Hrs: _____ / _____ / _____

Personal Training Session Goals:_____

_____

_____

_____

Instructor's Technique: _____

_____

_____

_____

Variations of Technique:_____

_____

_____

_____

_____

Combinations with Technique:_____

_____

_____

_____

_____

_____

_____

_____

Defending/Avoiding the Technique:_____

_____

_____

_____

_____

Reflect on your *wins*:_____

_____

_____

_____

_____

Reflect on your *losses*:_____

_____

_____

_____

_____

How can I improve:_____

_____

_____

_____

_____

_____

Date / Time/Total Hrs: _____ / _____ / _____

Personal Training Session Goals:_____

_____

_____

_____

Instructor's Technique: _____

_____

_____

_____

Variations of Technique:_____

_____

_____

_____

_____

Combinations with Technique:_____

_____

_____

_____

_____

_____

_____

Defending/Avoiding the Technique:_____

_____

_____

_____

_____

Reflect on your *wins*:_____

_____

_____

_____

_____

Reflect on your *losses*:_____

_____

_____

_____

_____

How can I improve:_____

_____

_____

_____

_____

_____

(1)Reflect on the last seven training entries. Identify how you've grown as a Jiu-Jitsu practitioner:_____

_____

_____

_____

_____

_____

_____

_____

_____

_____

What are your goals for the next seven training sessions:_____

_____

_____

_____

_____

_____

_____

_____

_____

Inspirational Jiu-Jitsu Quote

By:_____

Notes:

Date / Time/Total Hrs: _____ / _____ / _____

Personal Training Session Goals: _____

_____

_____

_____

Instructor's Technique: _____

_____

_____

_____

Variations of Technique: _____

_____

_____

_____

_____

Combinations with Technique: _____

_____

_____

_____

_____

_____

_____

_____

Defending/Avoiding the Technique:_____

_____

_____

_____

_____

Reflect on your *wins*:_____

_____

_____

_____

_____

Reflect on your *losses*:_____

_____

_____

_____

_____

_____

How can I improve:_____

_____

_____

_____

_____

_____

_____

Date / Time/Total Hrs: _____ / _____ / _____

Personal Training Session Goals:_____

_____

_____

_____

Instructor's Technique: _____

_____

_____

_____

Variations of Technique:_____

_____

_____

_____

_____

Combinations with Technique:_____

_____

_____

_____

_____

_____

_____

_____

Defending/Avoiding the Technique:_____

_____

_____

_____

_____

Reflect on your *wins*:_____

_____

_____

_____

_____

Reflect on your *losses*:_____

_____

_____

_____

_____

_____

How can I improve:_____

_____

_____

_____

_____

_____

_____

Date / Time/Total Hrs: _____ / _____ / _____

Personal Training Session Goals: _____

_____

_____

_____

Instructor's Technique: _____

_____

_____

_____

Variations of Technique: _____

_____

_____

_____

_____

Combinations with Technique: _____

_____

_____

_____

_____

_____

_____

_____

Defending/Avoiding the Technique:_____

_____

_____

_____

_____

Reflect on your *wins*:_____

_____

_____

_____

_____

Reflect on your *losses*:_____

_____

_____

_____

_____

_____

How can I improve:_____

_____

_____

_____

_____

_____

_____

Date / Time/Total Hrs: _____ / _____ / _____

Personal Training Session Goals:_____

_____

_____

_____

Instructor's Technique: _____

_____

_____

_____

Variations of Technique:_____

_____

_____

_____

_____

Combinations with Technique:_____

_____

_____

_____

_____

_____

_____

_____

Defending/Avoiding the Technique:_____

_____

_____

_____

_____

Reflect on your *wins*:_____

_____

_____

_____

_____

Reflect on your *losses*:_____

_____

_____

_____

_____

_____

How can I improve:_____

_____

_____

_____

_____

_____

Date / Time/Total Hrs: _____ / _____ / _____

Personal Training Session Goals: _____

_____

_____

_____

Instructor's Technique: _____

_____

_____

_____

Variations of Technique: _____

_____

_____

_____

_____

Combinations with Technique: _____

_____

_____

_____

_____

_____

_____

_____

Defending/Avoiding the Technique:_____

_____

_____

_____

_____

Reflect on your *wins*:_____

_____

_____

_____

_____

Reflect on your *losses*:_____

_____

_____

_____

_____

How can I improve:_____

_____

_____

_____

_____

_____

_____

Date / Time/Total Hrs: _____ / _____ / _____

Personal Training Session Goals:_____

_____

_____

_____

Instructor's Technique: _____

_____

_____

_____

Variations of Technique:_____

_____

_____

_____

_____

Combinations with Technique:_____

_____

_____

_____

_____

_____

_____

_____

Defending/Avoiding the Technique:_____

_____

_____

_____

_____

Reflect on your *wins*:_____

_____

_____

_____

_____

Reflect on your *losses*:_____

_____

_____

_____

_____

_____

How can I improve:_____

_____

_____

_____

_____

_____

_____

Date / Time/Total Hrs: _____ / _____ / _____

Personal Training Session Goals:_____

_____

_____

_____

Instructor's Technique: _____

_____

_____

_____

Variations of Technique:_____

_____

_____

_____

_____

Combinations with Technique:_____

_____

_____

_____

_____

_____

_____

Defending/Avoiding the Technique:_____

_____

_____

_____

_____

Reflect on your *wins*:_____

_____

_____

_____

_____

Reflect on your *losses*:_____

_____

_____

_____

_____

How can I improve:_____

_____

_____

_____

_____

_____

(2)Reflect on the last seven training entries. Identify how you've grown as a Jiu-Jitsu practitioner:_____

_____
_____
_____
_____
_____
_____
_____
_____
_____

What are your goals for the next seven training sessions:_____

_____
_____
_____
_____
_____
_____
_____
_____

Inspirational Jiu-Jitsu Quote

By:_____

Notes:

41

Date / Time/Total Hrs: _____ / _____ / _____

Personal Training Session Goals: _____

_____

_____

_____

Instructor's Technique: _____

_____

_____

_____

Variations of Technique: _____

_____

_____

_____

_____

Combinations with Technique: _____

_____

_____

_____

_____

_____

_____

_____

Defending/Avoiding the Technique:_____

_____

_____

_____

_____

Reflect on your _wins_:_____

_____

_____

_____

_____

Reflect on your _losses_:_____

_____

_____

_____

_____

How can I improve:_____

_____

_____

_____

_____

_____

Date / Time/Total Hrs: _____ / _____ / _____

Personal Training Session Goals: _____

_____

_____

_____

Instructor's Technique: _____

_____

_____

_____

Variations of Technique: _____

_____

_____

_____

_____

Combinations with Technique: _____

_____

_____

_____

_____

_____

_____

Defending/Avoiding the Technique:_____

_____

_____

_____

_____

Reflect on your *wins*:_____

_____

_____

_____

_____

Reflect on your *losses*:_____

_____

_____

_____

_____

_____

How can I improve:_____

_____

_____

_____

_____

_____

Date / Time/Total Hrs: _____ / _____ / _____

Personal Training Session Goals: _____

_____

_____

_____

Instructor's Technique: _____

_____

_____

_____

Variations of Technique: _____

_____

_____

_____

_____

Combinations with Technique: _____

_____

_____

_____

_____

_____

_____

_____

Defending/Avoiding the Technique:_____

_____

_____

_____

_____

Reflect on your _wins_:_____

_____

_____

_____

_____

Reflect on your _losses_:_____

_____

_____

_____

_____

How can I improve:_____

_____

_____

_____

_____

_____

Date / Time/Total Hrs: _____ / _____ / _____

Personal Training Session Goals:_____

_____

_____

_____

Instructor's Technique: _____

_____

_____

_____

Variations of Technique:_____

_____

_____

_____

_____

Combinations with Technique:_____

_____

_____

_____

_____

_____

_____

Defending/Avoiding the Technique:_____

_____

_____

_____

_____

Reflect on your *wins*:_____

_____

_____

_____

_____

Reflect on your *losses*:_____

_____

_____

_____

_____

How can I improve:_____

_____

_____

_____

_____

_____

_____

Date / Time/Total Hrs: _____ / _____ / _____

Personal Training Session Goals:_____

_____

_____

_____

Instructor's Technique: _____

_____

_____

_____

Variations of Technique:_____

_____

_____

_____

_____

Combinations with Technique:_____

_____

_____

_____

_____

_____

_____

_____

Defending/Avoiding the Technique:_____

_____
_____
_____
_____

Reflect on your *wins*:_____

_____
_____
_____
_____

Reflect on your *losses*:_____

_____
_____
_____
_____

How can I improve:_____

_____
_____
_____
_____
_____
_____

Date / Time/Total Hrs: _____ / _____ / _____

Personal Training Session Goals: _____

_____

_____

_____

Instructor's Technique: _____

_____

_____

_____

Variations of Technique: _____

_____

_____

_____

_____

Combinations with Technique: _____

_____

_____

_____

_____

_____

_____

_____

Defending/Avoiding the Technique:_____

_____

_____

_____

_____

Reflect on your *wins*:_____

_____

_____

_____

_____

Reflect on your *losses*:_____

_____

_____

_____

_____

_____

How can I improve:_____

_____

_____

_____

_____

_____

_____

Date / Time/Total Hrs: _____ / _____ / _____

Personal Training Session Goals: _____

_____

_____

_____

Instructor's Technique: _____

_____

_____

_____

Variations of Technique: _____

_____

_____

_____

_____

Combinations with Technique: _____

_____

_____

_____

_____

_____

_____

_____

Defending/Avoiding the Technique:_____

_____

_____

_____

_____

Reflect on your *wins*:_____

_____

_____

_____

_____

Reflect on your *losses*:_____

_____

_____

_____

_____

_____

How can I improve:_____

_____

_____

_____

_____

_____

_____

(3)Reflect on the last seven training entries. Identify how you've grown as a Jiu-Jitsu practitioner:_____

_____

_____

_____

_____

_____

_____

_____

_____

_____

What are your goals for the next seven training sessions:_____

_____

_____

_____

_____

_____

_____

_____

Inspirational Jiu-Jitsu Quote

By:_____

Notes:

Date / Time/Total Hrs: _____ / _____ / _____

Personal Training Session Goals: _____

_____

_____

_____

Instructor's Technique: _____

_____

_____

_____

Variations of Technique: _____

_____

_____

_____

_____

Combinations with Technique: _____

_____

_____

_____

_____

_____

_____

_____

Defending/Avoiding the Technique:_____

_____

_____

_____

_____

Reflect on your *wins*:_____

_____

_____

_____

_____

Reflect on your *losses*:_____

_____

_____

_____

_____

_____

How can I improve:_____

_____

_____

_____

_____

_____

Date / Time/Total Hrs: _____ / _____ / _____

Personal Training Session Goals:_____

_____

_____

_____

Instructor's Technique: _____

_____

_____

_____

Variations of Technique:_____

_____

_____

_____

_____

Combinations with Technique:_____

_____

_____

_____

_____

_____

_____

_____

Defending/Avoiding the Technique:_____

_____

_____

_____

_____

Reflect on your *wins*:_____

_____

_____

_____

_____

Reflect on your *losses*:_____

_____

_____

_____

_____

How can I improve:_____

_____

_____

_____

_____

_____

Date / Time/Total Hrs: _____ / _____ / _____

Personal Training Session Goals:_____

_____

_____

_____

Instructor's Technique: _____

_____

_____

_____

Variations of Technique:_____

_____

_____

_____

_____

Combinations with Technique:_____

_____

_____

_____

_____

_____

_____

_____

Defending/Avoiding the Technique:_____

_____

_____

_____

_____

Reflect on your *wins*:_____

_____

_____

_____

_____

Reflect on your *losses*:_____

_____

_____

_____

_____

How can I improve:_____

_____

_____

_____

_____

_____

_____

Date / Time/Total Hrs: _____ / _____ / _____

Personal Training Session Goals: _____

_____

_____

_____

Instructor's Technique: _____

_____

_____

_____

Variations of Technique: _____

_____

_____

_____

_____

Combinations with Technique: _____

_____

_____

_____

_____

_____

_____

_____

Defending/Avoiding the Technique:_____

_____

_____

_____

_____

Reflect on your _wins_:_____

_____

_____

_____

_____

Reflect on your _losses_:_____

_____

_____

_____

_____

How can I improve:_____

_____

_____

_____

_____

_____

Date / Time/Total Hrs: _____ / _____ / _____

Personal Training Session Goals: _____

_____

_____

_____

Instructor's Technique: _____

_____

_____

_____

Variations of Technique: _____

_____

_____

_____

_____

Combinations with Technique: _____

_____

_____

_____

_____

_____

_____

Defending/Avoiding the Technique:_____

_____

_____

_____

_____

Reflect on your *wins*:_____

_____

_____

_____

_____

Reflect on your *losses*:_____

_____

_____

_____

_____

_____

How can I improve:_____

_____

_____

_____

_____

_____

_____

Date / Time/Total Hrs: _____ / _____ / _____

Personal Training Session Goals:_____

_____

_____

_____

Instructor's Technique: _____

_____

_____

_____

Variations of Technique:_____

_____

_____

_____

_____

Combinations with Technique:_____

_____

_____

_____

_____

_____

_____

Defending/Avoiding the Technique:_____

_____

_____

_____

_____

Reflect on your *wins*:_____

_____

_____

_____

_____

Reflect on your *losses*:_____

_____

_____

_____

_____

_____

How can I improve:_____

_____

_____

_____

_____

_____

_____

Date / Time/Total Hrs: _____ / _____ / _____

Personal Training Session Goals: _____

_____

_____

_____

Instructor's Technique: _____

_____

_____

_____

Variations of Technique: _____

_____

_____

_____

_____

Combinations with Technique: _____

_____

_____

_____

_____

_____

_____

Defending/Avoiding the Technique:_____

_____

_____

_____

_____

Reflect on your *wins*:_____

_____

_____

_____

_____

Reflect on your *losses*:_____

_____

_____

_____

_____

_____

How can I improve:_____

_____

_____

_____

_____

_____

(4)Reflect on the last seven training entries. Identify how you've grown as a Jiu-Jitsu practitioner:_____

_____
_____
_____
_____
_____
_____
_____
_____

What are your goals for the next seven training sessions:_____

_____
_____
_____
_____
_____
_____
_____

Inspirational Jiu-Jitsu Quote

By:_____

Notes:

Date / Time/Total Hrs: _____ / _____ / _____

Personal Training Session Goals: _____

_____

_____

_____

Instructor's Technique: _____

_____

_____

_____

Variations of Technique: _____

_____

_____

_____

_____

Combinations with Technique: _____

_____

_____

_____

_____

_____

_____

_____

Defending/Avoiding the Technique:_____

_____

_____

_____

_____

Reflect on your *wins*:_____

_____

_____

_____

_____

Reflect on your *losses*:_____

_____

_____

_____

_____

_____

How can I improve:_____

_____

_____

_____

_____

_____

_____

Date / Time/Total Hrs: _____ / _____ / _____

Personal Training Session Goals:_____

_____

_____

_____

Instructor's Technique: _____

_____

_____

_____

Variations of Technique:_____

_____

_____

_____

_____

Combinations with Technique:_____

_____

_____

_____

_____

_____

_____

_____

Defending/Avoiding the Technique:_____

_____

_____

_____

_____

Reflect on your *wins*:_____

_____

_____

_____

_____

Reflect on your *losses*:_____

_____

_____

_____

_____

_____

How can I improve:_____

_____

_____

_____

_____

_____

_____

Date / Time/Total Hrs: _____ / _____ / _____

Personal Training Session Goals:_____

_____

_____

_____

Instructor's Technique: _____

_____

_____

_____

Variations of Technique:_____

_____

_____

_____

_____

Combinations with Technique:_____

_____

_____

_____

_____

_____

_____

_____

Defending/Avoiding the Technique:_____

_____

_____

_____

_____

Reflect on your *wins*:_____

_____

_____

_____

_____

Reflect on your *losses*:_____

_____

_____

_____

_____

_____

How can I improve:_____

_____

_____

_____

_____

_____

_____

Date / Time/Total Hrs: _____ / _____ / _____

Personal Training Session Goals:_____

_____

_____

_____

Instructor's Technique: _____

_____

_____

_____

Variations of Technique:_____

_____

_____

_____

_____

Combinations with Technique:_____

_____

_____

_____

_____

_____

_____

_____

Defending/Avoiding the Technique:_____

_____

_____

_____

_____

Reflect on your *wins*:_____

_____

_____

_____

_____

Reflect on your *losses*:_____

_____

_____

_____

_____

_____

How can I improve:_____

_____

_____

_____

_____

_____

_____

Date / Time/Total Hrs: _____ / _____ / _____

Personal Training Session Goals: _____

_____

_____

_____

Instructor's Technique: _____

_____

_____

_____

Variations of Technique: _____

_____

_____

_____

_____

Combinations with Technique: _____

_____

_____

_____

_____

_____

_____

_____

Defending/Avoiding the Technique:_____

_____

_____

_____

_____

Reflect on your *wins*:_____

_____

_____

_____

_____

Reflect on your *losses*:_____

_____

_____

_____

_____

How can I improve:_____

_____

_____

_____

_____

_____

Date / Time/Total Hrs: _____ / _____ / _____

Personal Training Session Goals: _____

_____

_____

_____

Instructor's Technique: _____

_____

_____

_____

Variations of Technique: _____

_____

_____

_____

_____

Combinations with Technique: _____

_____

_____

_____

_____

_____

_____

_____

Defending/Avoiding the Technique:_____

_____

_____

_____

_____

Reflect on your *wins*:_____

_____

_____

_____

_____

Reflect on your *losses*:_____

_____

_____

_____

_____

How can I improve:_____

_____

_____

_____

_____

_____

Date / Time/Total Hrs: _____ / _____ / _____

Personal Training Session Goals:_____

_____

_____

_____

Instructor's Technique: _____

_____

_____

_____

Variations of Technique:_____

_____

_____

_____

_____

Combinations with Technique:_____

_____

_____

_____

_____

_____

_____

_____

Defending/Avoiding the Technique:_____

_____

_____

_____

_____

Reflect on your *wins*:_____

_____

_____

_____

_____

Reflect on your *losses*:_____

_____

_____

_____

_____

How can I improve:_____

_____

_____

_____

_____

_____

_____

(5)Reflect on the last seven training entries. Identify how you've grown as a Jiu-Jitsu practitioner:_____

_____
_____
_____
_____
_____
_____
_____
_____
_____

What are your goals for the next seven training sessions:_____

_____
_____
_____
_____
_____
_____
_____
_____

Inspirational Jiu-Jitsu Quote

By:_____

Notes:

Date / Time/Total Hrs: _____ / _____ / _____

Personal Training Session Goals: _____

_____

_____

_____

Instructor's Technique: _____

_____

_____

_____

Variations of Technique: _____

_____

_____

_____

_____

Combinations with Technique: _____

_____

_____

_____

_____

_____

_____

Defending/Avoiding the Technique:_____

_____

_____

_____

_____

Reflect on your *wins*:_____

_____

_____

_____

_____

Reflect on your *losses*:_____

_____

_____

_____

_____

_____

How can I improve:_____

_____

_____

_____

_____

_____

_____

Date / Time/Total Hrs: _____ / _____ / _____

Personal Training Session Goals:_____

_____

_____

_____

Instructor's Technique: _____

_____

_____

_____

Variations of Technique:_____

_____

_____

_____

_____

Combinations with Technique:_____

_____

_____

_____

_____

_____

_____

Defending/Avoiding the Technique:_____

_____

_____

_____

_____

Reflect on your _wins_:_____

_____

_____

_____

_____

Reflect on your _losses_:_____

_____

_____

_____

_____

How can I improve:_____

_____

_____

_____

_____

_____

Date / Time/Total Hrs: _____ / _____ / _____

Personal Training Session Goals:_____

_____

_____

_____

Instructor's Technique: _____

_____

_____

_____

Variations of Technique:_____

_____

_____

_____

_____

Combinations with Technique:_____

_____

_____

_____

_____

_____

_____

_____

Defending/Avoiding the Technique:_____

_____

_____

_____

_____

Reflect on your *wins*:_____

_____

_____

_____

_____

Reflect on your *losses*:_____

_____

_____

_____

_____

How can I improve:_____

_____

_____

_____

_____

_____

_____

Date / Time/Total Hrs: _____ / _____ / _____

Personal Training Session Goals:_____

_____

_____

_____

Instructor's Technique: _____

_____

_____

_____

Variations of Technique:_____

_____

_____

_____

_____

Combinations with Technique:_____

_____

_____

_____

_____

_____

_____

_____

Defending/Avoiding the Technique:_____

_____

_____

_____

_____

Reflect on your *wins*:_____

_____

_____

_____

_____

Reflect on your *losses*:_____

_____

_____

_____

_____

How can I improve:_____

_____

_____

_____

_____

_____

Date / Time/Total Hrs: _____ / _____ / _____

Personal Training Session Goals:_____

_____

_____

_____

Instructor's Technique: _____

_____

_____

_____

Variations of Technique:_____

_____

_____

_____

_____

Combinations with Technique:_____

_____

_____

_____

_____

_____

_____

Defending/Avoiding the Technique:_____

_____

_____

_____

_____

Reflect on your *wins*:_____

_____

_____

_____

_____

Reflect on your *losses*:_____

_____

_____

_____

_____

How can I improve:_____

_____

_____

_____

_____

_____

Date / Time/Total Hrs: _____ / _____ / _____

Personal Training Session Goals:_____

_____

_____

_____

Instructor's Technique: _____

_____

_____

_____

Variations of Technique:_____

_____

_____

_____

_____

Combinations with Technique:_____

_____

_____

_____

_____

_____

_____

Defending/Avoiding the Technique:_____

_____

_____

_____

_____

Reflect on your *wins*:_____

_____

_____

_____

_____

Reflect on your *losses*:_____

_____

_____

_____

_____

How can I improve:_____

_____

_____

_____

_____

_____

Date / Time/Total Hrs: _____ / _____ / _____

Personal Training Session Goals: _____

_____

_____

_____

Instructor's Technique: _____

_____

_____

_____

Variations of Technique: _____

_____

_____

_____

_____

Combinations with Technique: _____

_____

_____

_____

_____

_____

_____

_____

Defending/Avoiding the Technique:_____

_____

_____

_____

_____

Reflect on your *wins*:_____

_____

_____

_____

_____

Reflect on your *losses*:_____

_____

_____

_____

_____

How can I improve:_____

_____

_____

_____

_____

_____

(6)*Reflect* on the last seven training entries. Identify how you've grown as a Jiu-Jitsu practitioner:_____

_____
_____
_____
_____
_____
_____
_____
_____
_____

What are your goals for the next seven training sessions:_____

_____
_____
_____
_____
_____
_____
_____
_____

Inspirational Jiu-Jitsu Quote

By:_____

Notes:

Date / Time/Total Hrs: _____ / _____ / _____

Personal Training Session Goals:_____

_____

_____

_____

Instructor's Technique: _____

_____

_____

_____

Variations of Technique:_____

_____

_____

_____

_____

Combinations with Technique:_____

_____

_____

_____

_____

_____

_____

Defending/Avoiding the Technique:_____

_____

_____

_____

_____

Reflect on your _wins_:_____

_____

_____

_____

_____

Reflect on your _losses_:_____

_____

_____

_____

_____

How can I improve:_____

_____

_____

_____

_____

_____

Date / Time/Total Hrs: _____ / _____ / _____

Personal Training Session Goals:_____

_____

_____

_____

Instructor's Technique: _____

_____

_____

_____

Variations of Technique:_____

_____

_____

_____

_____

Combinations with Technique:_____

_____

_____

_____

_____

_____

_____

_____

Defending/Avoiding the Technique:_____

_____

_____

_____

_____

Reflect on your *wins*:_____

_____

_____

_____

_____

Reflect on your *losses*:_____

_____

_____

_____

_____

_____

How can I improve:_____

_____

_____

_____

_____

_____

_____

Date / Time/Total Hrs: _____ / _____ / _____

Personal Training Session Goals: _____

_____

_____

_____

Instructor's Technique: _____

_____

_____

_____

Variations of Technique: _____

_____

_____

_____

_____

Combinations with Technique: _____

_____

_____

_____

_____

_____

_____

_____

Defending/Avoiding the Technique:_____

_____

_____

_____

_____

Reflect on your *wins*:_____

_____

_____

_____

_____

Reflect on your *losses*:_____

_____

_____

_____

_____

_____

How can I improve:_____

_____

_____

_____

_____

_____

_____

Date / Time/Total Hrs: _____ / _____ / _____

Personal Training Session Goals:_____

_____

_____

_____

Instructor's Technique: _____

_____

_____

_____

Variations of Technique:_____

_____

_____

_____

_____

Combinations with Technique:_____

_____

_____

_____

_____

_____

_____

_____

Defending/Avoiding the Technique:_____

_____

_____

_____

_____

Reflect on your *wins*:_____

_____

_____

_____

_____

Reflect on your *losses*:_____

_____

_____

_____

_____

How can I improve:_____

_____

_____

_____

_____

_____

_____

Date / Time/Total Hrs: _____ / _____ / _____

Personal Training Session Goals:_____

_____

_____

_____

Instructor's Technique: _____

_____

_____

_____

Variations of Technique:_____

_____

_____

_____

_____

Combinations with Technique:_____

_____

_____

_____

_____

_____

_____

Defending/Avoiding the Technique:_____

_____

_____

_____

_____

Reflect on your *wins*:_____

_____

_____

_____

_____

Reflect on your *losses*:_____

_____

_____

_____

_____

How can I improve:_____

_____

_____

_____

_____

_____

Date / Time/Total Hrs: _____ / _____ / _____

Personal Training Session Goals:_____

_____

_____

_____

Instructor's Technique: _____

_____

_____

_____

Variations of Technique:_____

_____

_____

_____

_____

Combinations with Technique:_____

_____

_____

_____

_____

_____

_____

_____

Defending/Avoiding the Technique:_____

_____

_____

_____

_____

Reflect on your *wins*:_____

_____

_____

_____

_____

Reflect on your *losses*:_____

_____

_____

_____

_____

How can I improve:_____

_____

_____

_____

_____

_____

_____

Date / Time/Total Hrs: _____ / _____ / _____

Personal Training Session Goals:_____

_____

_____

_____

Instructor's Technique: _____

_____

_____

_____

Variations of Technique:_____

_____

_____

_____

_____

Combinations with Technique:_____

_____

_____

_____

_____

_____

_____

_____

Defending/Avoiding the Technique:_____

_____

_____

_____

_____

Reflect on your *wins*:_____

_____

_____

_____

_____

Reflect on your *losses*:_____

_____

_____

_____

_____

_____

How can I improve:_____

_____

_____

_____

_____

_____

_____

(7)Reflect on the last seven training entries. Identify how you've grown as a Jiu-Jitsu practitioner:_____

_____

_____

_____

_____

_____

_____

_____

_____

_____

What are your goals for the next seven training sessions:_____

_____

_____

_____

_____

_____

_____

_____

Inspirational Jiu-Jitsu Quote

By:_____

Notes:

121

Date / Time/Total Hrs: _____ / _____ / _____

Personal Training Session Goals:_____

_____

_____

_____

Instructor's Technique: _____

_____

_____

_____

Variations of Technique:_____

_____

_____

_____

_____

Combinations with Technique:_____

_____

_____

_____

_____

_____

_____

_____

Defending/Avoiding the Technique:_____

_____

_____

_____

_____

Reflect on your *wins*:_____

_____

_____

_____

_____

Reflect on your *losses*:_____

_____

_____

_____

_____

How can I improve:_____

_____

_____

_____

_____

_____

_____

Date / Time/Total Hrs: _____ / _____ / _____

Personal Training Session Goals:_____

_____

_____

_____

Instructor's Technique: _____

_____

_____

_____

Variations of Technique:_____

_____

_____

_____

_____

Combinations with Technique:_____

_____

_____

_____

_____

_____

_____

_____

Defending/Avoiding the Technique:_____

_____

_____

_____

_____

Reflect on your *wins*:_____

_____

_____

_____

_____

Reflect on your *losses*:_____

_____

_____

_____

_____

How can I improve:_____

_____

_____

_____

_____

_____

_____

Date / Time/Total Hrs: _____ / _____ / _____

Personal Training Session Goals: _____

_____

_____

_____

Instructor's Technique: _____

_____

_____

_____

Variations of Technique: _____

_____

_____

_____

_____

Combinations with Technique: _____

_____

_____

_____

_____

_____

_____

Defending/Avoiding the Technique:_____

_____

_____

_____

_____

Reflect on your *wins*:_____

_____

_____

_____

_____

Reflect on your *losses*:_____

_____

_____

_____

_____

_____

How can I improve:_____

_____

_____

_____

_____

_____

_____

Date / Time/Total Hrs: _____ / _____ / _____

Personal Training Session Goals:_____

_____

_____

_____

Instructor's Technique: _____

_____

_____

_____

Variations of Technique:_____

_____

_____

_____

_____

Combinations with Technique:_____

_____

_____

_____

_____

_____

_____

_____

Defending/Avoiding the Technique:_____

_____

_____

_____

_____

Reflect on your *wins*:_____

_____

_____

_____

_____

Reflect on your *losses*:_____

_____

_____

_____

_____

How can I improve:_____

_____

_____

_____

_____

_____

_____

Date / Time/Total Hrs: _____ / _____ / _____

Personal Training Session Goals: _____

_____

_____

_____

Instructor's Technique: _____

_____

_____

_____

Variations of Technique: _____

_____

_____

_____

_____

Combinations with Technique: _____

_____

_____

_____

_____

_____

_____

Defending/Avoiding the Technique:_____

_____

_____

_____

_____

Reflect on your *wins*:_____

_____

_____

_____

_____

Reflect on your *losses*:_____

_____

_____

_____

_____

_____

How can I improve:_____

_____

_____

_____

_____

_____

_____

Date / Time/Total Hrs: _____ / _____ / _____

Personal Training Session Goals: _____

_____

_____

_____

Instructor's Technique: _____

_____

_____

_____

Variations of Technique: _____

_____

_____

_____

_____

Combinations with Technique: _____

_____

_____

_____

_____

_____

_____

Defending/Avoiding the Technique:_____

_____

_____

_____

_____

Reflect on your *wins*:_____

_____

_____

_____

_____

Reflect on your *losses*:_____

_____

_____

_____

_____

How can I improve:_____

_____

_____

_____

_____

_____

Date / Time/Total Hrs: _____ / _____ / _____

Personal Training Session Goals:_____

_____

_____

_____

Instructor's Technique: _____

_____

_____

_____

Variations of Technique:_____

_____

_____

_____

_____

Combinations with Technique:_____

_____

_____

_____

_____

_____

_____

Defending/Avoiding the Technique:_____

_____

_____

_____

_____

Reflect on your *wins*:_____

_____

_____

_____

_____

Reflect on your *losses*:_____

_____

_____

_____

_____

How can I improve:_____

_____

_____

_____

_____

_____

_____

(8)*Reflect* on the last seven training entries. Identify how you've grown as a Jiu-Jitsu practitioner:_____

_____

_____

_____

_____

_____

_____

_____

_____

What are your goals for the next seven training sessions:_____

_____

_____

_____

_____

_____

_____

_____

Inspirational Jiu-Jitsu Quote

By:_____

Notes:

My Jiu-Jitsu Flowchart

Imagine yourself in a fight from start to finish. Describe as many details and scenarios as possible. As you grow in Jiu-Jitsu, your flow chart will increase with an amazing amount of scenarios and your body will flow through them naturally. Reflect on your flow chart during your Jiu-Jitsu journey to monitor your growth and identify weaknesses.

Distance control:_____

_____

_____

Opponent's body style:_____

_____

Opponent's fight style:_____

_____

_____

Take down:_____

_____

_____

_____

_____

Take down variations:_____

_____

_____

_____

_____

_____

Ground Position:(top/bottom)_____

_____

_____

_____

_____

_____

Scramble:_____

_____

_____

_____

Control:_____

_____

_____

_____

Transitions:_____

_____

_____

_____

Set ups:_____

_____

_____

_____

Combinations:_____

_____

_____

_____

_____

_____

Finish:_____

_____

_____

_____

_____

Flowchart 1

Draw a flowchart for easy reference.

Flowchart 2:

Flowchart 3:

*My Specialty Position:*_____

Maintaining the position:_____
_____
_____
_____

Move 1:_____
_____
_____
_____

Move 2:_____
_____
_____
_____

Move 3:_____
_____
_____
_____

Move 4:_____
_____
_____
_____

Move 5:_____
_____
_____
_____

Combos that have worked the best:

1, 2, 3, 4 / 3, 1, 4, 2 etc. _____
_____

Escapes:_____

_____
_____
_____
_____
_____
_____
_____
_____
_____
_____
_____
_____
_____
_____
_____
_____
_____
_____
_____
_____
_____
_____
_____
_____
_____
_____
_____
_____
_____
_____

Escapes continued:_____

_____

_____

_____

_____

_____

_____

_____

_____

_____

_____

_____

_____

_____

_____

_____

_____

_____

_____

_____

_____

_____

_____

_____

_____

_____

_____

_____

_____

_____

_____

*Personal Notes:*_____

_____
_____
_____
_____
_____
_____
_____
_____
_____
_____
_____
_____
_____
_____
_____
_____
_____
_____
_____
_____
_____
_____
_____
_____
_____
_____
_____
_____
_____
_____

Reflections 1	
Reflections 2	
Reflections 3	
Reflections 4	
Reflections 5	
Reflections 6	
Reflections 7	
Reflections 8	
Total Hours	

Training Partners

Name   Belt Rank

How they helped your Jiu-Jitsu / Their specialty

Name   Belt Rank

How they helped your Jiu-Jitsu / Their specialty

Name   Belt Rank

How they helped your Jiu-Jitsu / Their specialty

Name   Belt Rank

How they helped your Jiu-Jitsu / Their specialty

Your Body

Your body will feel pain and power. Some days are better than others. They should be noted. Listen to your body and understand it.

Foods with energy:_____

_____

_____

_____

_____

Foods for recovery:_____

_____

_____

_____

_____

Drinks that replenish electrolytes:_____

_____

_____

Hours of sleep needed:_____

Training Schedule:_____

_____

_____

_____

Stretching:_____

_____

_____

_____

Meditation and Breathing exercises:_____

_____

_____

_____

Things that slow you down:_____

_____

_____

_____

_____

Distractions:_____

_____

_____

_____

Bad Habits:_____

_____

_____

_____

_____

_____

Records

Belt	Date	Instructor
White:	_____	_____
White 1:	_____	_____
White 2:	_____	_____
White 3:	_____	_____
White 4:	_____	_____
Blue:	_____	_____
Blue 1:	_____	_____
Blue 2:	_____	_____
Blue 3:	_____	_____
Blue 4:	_____	_____
Purple:	_____	_____
Purple 1:	_____	_____
Purple 2:	_____	_____
Purple 3:	_____	_____
Purple 4:	_____	_____

Belt	Date	Instructor
Brown:	_____	_____
Brown 1:	_____	_____
Brown 2:	_____	_____
Brown 3:	_____	_____
Brown 4:	_____	_____
Black:	_____	_____
Black 1:	_____	_____
Black 2:	_____	_____
Black 3:	_____	_____
Black 4:	_____	_____

Special Moments Detailed

_____

_____

_____

_____

_____

_____

_____

_____

Tournaments 1

Promoter:_____

Location:_____

Date:_____

Belt Rank:_____

Match 1 W/L, Opponent:_____

Match 2 W/L, Opponent:_____

Match 3 W/L, Opponent:_____

Match 4 W/L, Opponent:_____

Match 5 W/L, Opponent:_____

Final Place in Tournament: 1st, 2nd, 3rd or _____

Tournament Reflections:_____

_____

_____

_____

_____

_____

_____

_____

_____

_____

Tournaments 2

Promoter:_____

Location:_____

Date:_____

Belt Rank:_____

Match 1 W/L, Opponent:_____

Match 2 W/L, Opponent:_____

Match 3 W/L, Opponent:_____

Match 4 W/L, Opponent:_____

Match 5 W/L, Opponent:_____

Final Place in Tournament: 1st, 2nd, 3rd or _____

Tournament Reflections:_____

_____

_____

_____

_____

_____

_____

_____

_____

_____

Tournaments 3

Promoter:_____

Location:_____

Date:_____

Belt Rank:_____

Match 1 W/L, Opponent:_____

Match 2 W/L, Opponent:_____

Match 3 W/L, Opponent:_____

Match 4 W/L, Opponent:_____

Match 5 W/L, Opponent:_____

Final Place in Tournament: 1st, 2nd, 3rd or _____

Tournament Reflections:_____

_____

_____

_____

_____

_____

_____

_____

_____

Tournaments 4

Promoter:_____

Location:_____

Date:_____

Belt Rank:_____

Match 1 W/L, Opponent:_____

Match 2 W/L, Opponent:_____

Match 3 W/L, Opponent:_____

Match 4 W/L, Opponent:_____

Match 5 W/L, Opponent:_____

Final Place in Tournament: 1st, 2^{nd,} 3rd or _____

Tournament Reflections:_____

_____

_____

_____

_____

_____

_____

_____

_____

Goals

Weekly:_____

_____

_____

_____

_____

_____

Quarterly (3 months):_____

_____

_____

_____

Biannual (6 months):_____

_____

_____

_____

Annual and/or a Specific Goal:_____

_____

_____

_____

_____

_____

Directions:

1. Think, Train and fill out your Journal. As you fill out your journal, update your Table of Contents.

2. Reflect on your training experience to see the good and bad, what you have learned and what you need to do to get better?

3. Stay motivated and strong minded by writing quotes that have meaning to you and from people you admire.

4. Your Jiu-Jitsu flowchart can be of an entire fight as described in that chapter or start with a specialized position and master it.

5. Your flowchart reference is a visual tool to refresh your memory on the scenarios that you've already thought of. A simple reminder of some of the combinations that you've worked on.

6. Your specialized position should have a minimum of 5 options, otherwise it's not specialized. Everyone has 3 options from every position. Master 5 options and use

combinations of the 5 to dominate your opponent.

7. Every training session you will have to tap, escape and/or transition. Most of us have to tap. Remember your losses and begin to build options. Learn how to avoid and escape your trouble areas. Don't just leave class talking about your wins. Analyze your losses.

8. Personal notes can be used and formatted for whatever you want. Please inform the author of ways that may improve this journal.

9. Keep track of your accumulated time. It helps you see how much time has lapsed while learning specific techniques. This will help you hone in on your learning preferences. Sum your 7 sessions and account for them as one reflection. Add all your reflections together to see your total hours. Reflect on this journal and your jiu-jitsu journey.

10.   Training partners make the difference. Good or bad, they are needed. Say something positive that has helped your jiu-jitsu or you as a person.

11. Your body and how it feels are very important. Monitor your body for optimal performance. Feed it nutritious meals and allow it to rest. Fill out this chapter as part of being aware and to keep you on track.

12. Records are awesome to keep. It's a road map of where you've been. To reflect on your past will show you your future.

13. Not all practitioners have the ability to compete due to numerous legit reasons but this chapter is here to motivate you to try. If you are a regular in the circuit, fill it out and leave a trail of broken opponents.

14. All your short-term goals should lead to your mid-term goals and all your mid-term goals should lead to your long-term goals. Stay focused and keep your mind right. Get rid of the distractions and conquer your goals.

15. Directions, did you really read all the directions :) If so, you're on your way to becoming a champion. Do the things that others won't, so you can do the things that others can't.

16.   The index is for special places and subjects in the book that you may want to note.

17.   What is the history of Jiu-Jitsu? It's easier to remember if you research and write it down.

18.   Thank the author and tell a friend about this journal. Messing around a bit. Train smart, hard and safe. God Bless.

Best of luck to you my friend. See you on the mats!

About the Author

Primary (you)

_____

_____

_____

_____

_____

_____

_____

_____

_____

_____

_____

_____

_____

_____

_____

Secondary

Frank Anderson is a family man, engineer and Jiu-Jitsu practitioner. His training has been limited due to his career offshore. Needing to find a way to efficiently grow in his Jiu-Jitsu Journey, he created the Jiu-Jitsu Journal.

Index

Description	Page

Index

Description	Page
_____	____
_____	____
_____	____
_____	____
_____	____
_____	____
_____	____
_____	____
_____	____
_____	____
_____	____
_____	____
_____	____
_____	____
_____	____

Index

Description	Page
_____	_____
_____	_____
_____	_____
_____	_____
_____	_____
_____	_____
_____	_____
_____	_____
_____	_____
_____	_____
_____	_____
_____	_____
_____	_____
_____	_____
_____	_____
_____	_____

Index

Description	Page

History of Jiu-Jitsu

Proof

Made in the USA
Charleston, SC
24 September 2016